The Bourbon Show Presents…

Bourbon

Mixology

Vol. 4

50 Craft Distilleries
Share Signature Bourbon Cocktails

by
Colonel Steve Akley
&
Lee Ann Sciuto

The Bourbon Show Presents...
Bourbon Mixology, Vol. 4
50 Craft Distilleries Share Signature Bourbon Cocktails

Written by:
Colonel Steve Akley
& Lee Ann Sciuto

Published by:
S.A.P. Entertainment

To the #ABVNetworkCrew:

This one is dedicated to the ABV Network Crew, our most loyal fans… none of this is possible without you!

Introduction

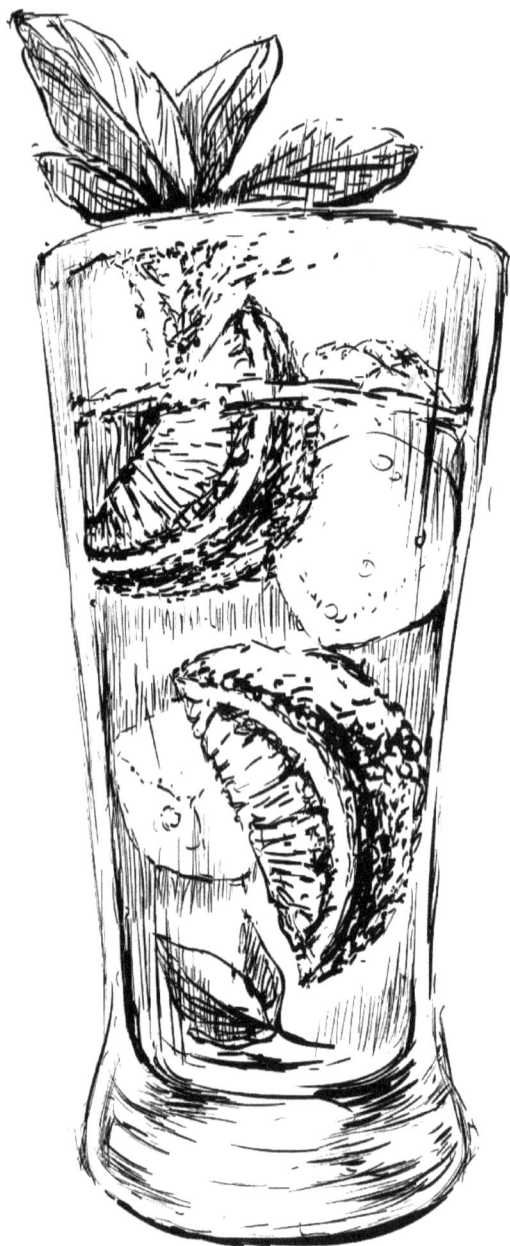

THE BOURBON SHOW

ABVNETWORK.COM

The Bourbon Show Presents…

Bourbon Mixology Vol. 4
50 Craft Distilleries Share Signature Bourbon Cocktails

Introduction by Colonel Steve Akley, Author

Think about what craft distillers are up against…

While mail order may account for a very small percentage of liquor sales, most revenue is going to be generated from retail outlets: traditional liquor stores, convenience stores, supermarkets, etc. On the shelves of those stores, the small craft distillers are forced to compete side-by-side with huge corporations that outspend them on advertising, have more resources at their disposal and likely have equipment, processes and the buying power to reduce costs.

The craft distiller, on the other hand, needs to get creative to capture potential customer's attention. One of the ways they do this is through the creation of unique cocktails using the bourbon they so painstakingly produce.

All of this comes together into a book featuring the signature bourbon cocktails of 50 craft distillers giving you 50 really great "bourbon forward" cocktails. While any bourbon can be substituted for the recipes you have here, I certainly would encourage you to seek out the brands when possible. I've been lucky enough to get to know many of them through interviews for my podcasts and **Bourbon Zeppelin**, my monthly bourbon magazine, and I can tell you these are passionate people and *almost* as much care went into creating these cocktails to feature their brands as the products that they make so you are going to love them. Mixing up these 50 cocktails is a journey… but a pretty fun one. I mean you've got a bourbon cocktail in your hand while you're doing it, right?

Okay… it's **Bourbon Mixology** time!

Cheers!

Table of Contents

The Signature Cocktails

2bar Spirits

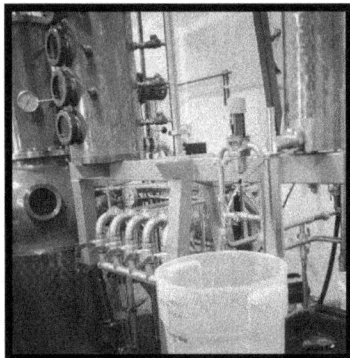

2960 4th Avenue South #106
Seattle, Washington 98134
(206) 402-4340

2barspirits.com
info@2barspirits.com

Established
2012

Leadership
Nathan Kaiser, Founder

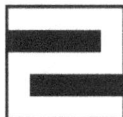

2bar Old Fashioned

Submitted by: Nathan Kaiser

Serve in a rocks glass

Ingredients:
- 1 teaspoon superfine sugar (or 1 sugar cube)
- 2 to 3 dashes Angostura bitters
- 2 ounces 2bar Bourbon
- Orange slice to garnish

Preparation:
1. Place all ingredients, other than orange slice, in a cocktail shaker with ice.
2. Shake vigorously for one minute.
3. Strain over ice.
4. Add orange slice.

2bar Old Fashioned

by 2bar Spirits

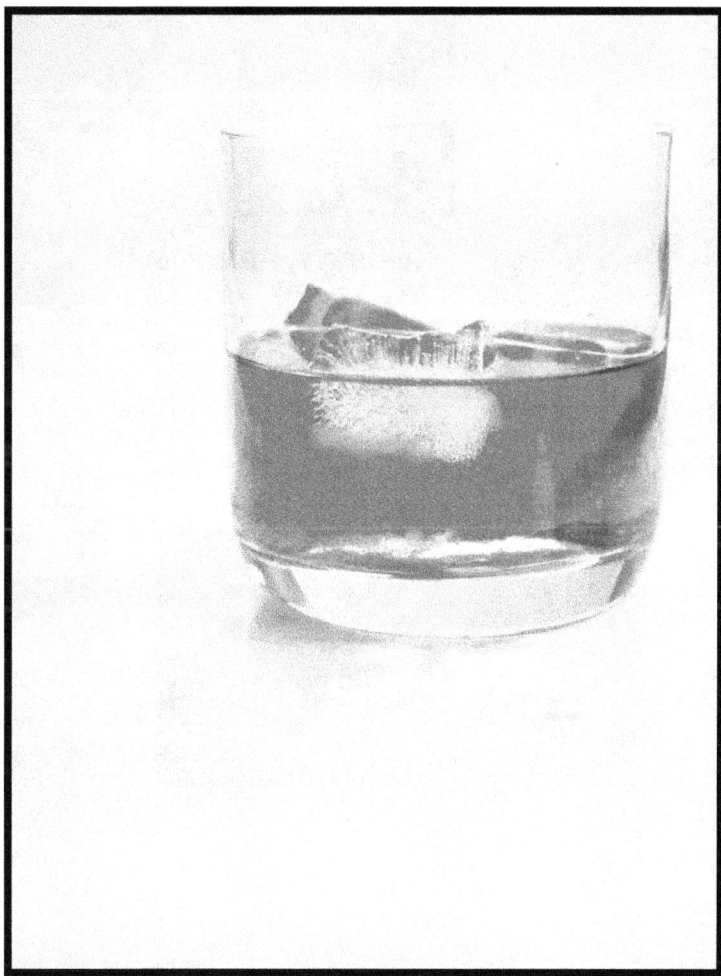

Big Escambia Spirits, LLC

Atmore, Alabama

Established
2014

Leadership
Seth Dettling, CEO/Head Distiller

Goat Feathers Up

A cocktail developed by acclaimed Big Escambia Spirits Head Mixologist Jeff Robinson.

Submitted by: Seth Dettling

Serve in a snifter

Ingredients:
- 1 ounce Dettling Bourbon
- ½ ounce St. Germain Elder Flower Liqueur
- ½ ounce Brentzen Apple Liqueur
- ½ ounce Tribuno Dry Vermouth or other premium dry vermouth
- ½ ounce simple syrup
- ¾ ounce lemon juice

Preparation:
1. Combine all ingredients into a cocktail shaker and add 1 cup of ice cubes.
2. Cover and shake hard for 20 seconds.
3. Strain into your favorite glass.
4. Garnish with a lemon slice or twist. Can be served on the rocks or straight up.

Goat Feathers Up

by Big Escambia Spirits, LLC

Boone County Distilling Co.

10601 Toebben Drive
Boone County, Kentucky 41051
(859) 282-6545

madebyghosts.com
info@boonedistilling.com

Established
2015

Leadership
Jack Wells, Gene Taft and Josh Quinn

Gold Miner's Ghost

When creator Molly Madden was first learning to isolate individual flavors within a bourbon, she was taught to taste with just a few simple things: cheese, dried fruit, toasted nuts, sorghum, and chocolate. The flavors of these foods reach and gratify nearly every part of our palate, and so, logically, adding them to a bourbon cocktail should only enhance that bourbon's flavors. Rich layers reveal themselves as Meletti curves around notes of caramelized sugars, creamy cocoa smooths out charred oak edges, dessert wine provides a soft landing for flavors of torched cherries, and fresh citrus plays up the sweet corn backbone of bourbon.

Submitted by: Molly Madden (creator) & Boone County Distilling

Serve in a coupe

Ingredients:
- 2 barspoons Amaro Meletti
- ½ ounce Tempus Fugit Creme de Cacao
- ½ ounce Quady's Batch 88 California Dessert Wine
- 2 ounces Boone Country Distilling Eighteen33
- One fresh swath of orange peel

Preparation:
1. Add all ingredients to a mixing glass and stir with ice until cool, but not ice cold.
2. Strain into a coupe.
3. Express a fresh orange peel over the top of the drink, and use the peel as a garnish.

Goldminer's Ghost

by Boone County Distilling Co.

Bouck Brothers Distilling

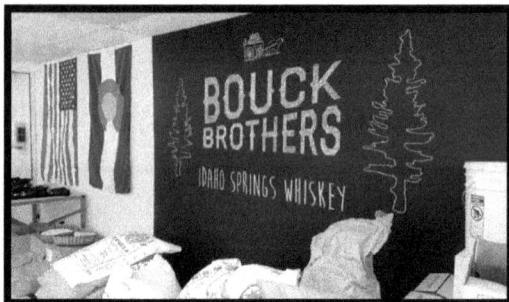

2731 Colorado Boulevard
Idaho Springs, Colorado 80452
(303) 567-2547

bouckbros.com
bouckbrothersdistilling@gmail.com

Established
2016

Leadership
Zak and Nick Bouck

Maple Bourbon Whiskey Sour

This cocktail has eased its fair share of disagreements between Zak Bouck and his wife, therefore has been affectionately nicknamed the "marriage counselor."

Submitted by: Zak and Jessica Bouck

Serve in a coupe

Ingredients:
- 2 ½ ounces bourbon
- ¾ ounce pure maple syrup
- Juice from half a lemon

Preparation:
1. Combine ingredients into a shaker with ice.
2. Shake.
3. Strain and serve.

Maple Bourbon Whiskey Sour

by Bouck Brothers Distilling

Bourbon 30 Crafts Spirits Distillery

130 South Water Street
Georgetown, Kentucky 40324
(859) 433-0801

itsbourbon30.com
scott@itsbourbon30.com

Established
2010

Leadership
Jeff Mattingly, Owner
Dominick Bizzaro, Owner

Black Cherry 30

Bourbon 30 Single Barrel has a cherry, cream flavor that is highlighted by this recipe. They wanted something that could incorporate a sparkling water to highlight the fact our distillery is located across from Royal Spring, which was the first water source used in the state of Kentucky for distilling.

Submitted by: Scott Pugh, New Product Director

Serve in a rocks glass

Ingredients:

- 4 bourbon-soaked black cherries
- 1 extra bourbon-soaked black cherry (for garnish)
- 1 ½ ounces Single Barrel Bourbon 30
- 1 teaspoon simple syrup
- ½ ounce freshly squeezed lemon juice
- Sparkling Ice (Black Cherry flavor)

Preparation:

1. Muddle black cherries that have been soaked in Bourbon 30 Single Barrel at the bottom of a cocktail shaker.
2. Add Bourbon 30 Single Barrel, simple syrup, and fresh lemon juice-shake.
3. Strain cocktail into a rocks glass with ice and add sparkling water.
4. Garnish with a lemon twist and a black cherry soaked in Bourbon 30 Single Barrel and serve.

Cockpit Craft Distillery

4893 Galley Road
Colorado Springs, Colorado 80915
(720) 299-0071

cockpitdistillery.com
calder@cockpitdistillery.com

Established
2014

Leadership
Calder Curtis

Pre-Flight (Old Fashioned)

Submitted by: Calder Curtis

Serve in a rocks glass

Ingredients:
- 1 ½ ounces P-51 Whiskey
- ¾ ounce Grade A organic maple syrup
- Orange slice
- Orange peel
- Luxardo cherry
- Ice sphere

Preparation:
1. On a granite cutting board, torch a small chunk of maple wood, then put out the wood by smothering it out with a rocks glass sprayed with water (to allow a contact point for the smoke).
2. Wait approximately 30 seconds, then, turn the glass over.
3. While spinning the glass, wash the smoke off the sides of the glass with the whiskey.
4. Add the Grade A organic maple syrup.
5. Using a channel knife, peel about six to eight inches of orange peel, cut into strips and add to the glass.
6. Add a large ice ball and garnish with a luxardo cherry, a slice of orange and enjoy.

Pre-Flight

by Cockpit Craft Distillery

Copper Fiddle Distillery

532 West Illinois Route 22, Suite 110
Lake Zurich, Illinois 60047
(847) 847-7609

copperfiddledistillery.com
nancy@copperfiddle.com

Established
2013

Leadership
Jose Hernandez
Fred Robinson

Basil Old Fashioned

Submitted by: Kristin Brandt, Bartender

Serve in a rocks glass

Ingredients:
- 3 basil leaves
- 1 orange slice
- ¼ ounce simple syrup
- 1 ½ ounces Copper Fiddle Bourbon
- 2 splashes soda water
- 2 dashes of orange bitters

Preparation:
1. Muddle orange slice, basil, and simple syrup in a cocktail shaker.
2. Poor into a rocks glass.
3. Add bourbon, soda water, and top with bitters.

Basil Old Fashioned

by Copper Fiddle Distillery

Cutwater Spirits

9750 Distribution Avenue
San Diego, California 92121
(858) 672-3848

cutwaterspirits.com

Established
2017

Dark Thorne

Submitted by: Cutwater Spirits

Serve in a coupe

Ingredients:
- 1 ½ ounces Devil's Share Bourbon
- ½ ounce Linie Aquavit
- ¾ ounce Punt e Mes
- ¼ ounce Giffard Apricot Liqueur
- 2 dashes Angostura Bitters
- Orange zest

Preparation:
1. Combine ingredients in a coupe.
2. Stir.
3. Garnish with a strip of orange peel.
4. Serve.

Dark Thorne

by Cutwater Spirits

Dark Corner Distillery

14 South Main Street
Greenville, South Carolina 29601
(864) 631-1144

darkcornerdistillery.com
info@darkcornerdistillery.com

Established
2011

Leadership
Joe Fenten, Founder

GREENVILLE, SOUTH CAROLINA

Bourbon Peach Smash

Submitted by: Joe Fenten

Serve in a julep cup

Ingredients:
- 2 ounces Lewis Redmond Bourbon
- 1 ounce of peach purée
- ½ ounce simple syrup
- 1 peach slice
- 3 mint leaves

Preparation:
1. In a mixing glass, muddle the mint and simple syrup.
2. Add ice, Lewis Redmond Bourbon and peach purée. Shake and strain into an ice-filled rocks glass.
3. Garnish with a peach slice.

Detroit City Distillery

2462 Riopelle Street
Detroit, Michigan 48207
(313) 338-3760

detroitcitydistillery.com
tastingroom@detroitcitydistillery.com

Established
2014

Leadership
John Paul Jerome, Master Distiller
Cole Levy, General Manager/Beverage Director

Orange You Glad

This cocktail came to fruition thanks to a dream by Cole Levy, General Manager/Beverage Director for Detroit City Distillery. After much trial and error, she perfected the pickled then candied orange and built from there to create a drink that tastes like fall. The flavors of all spice, cloves and cinnamon are prominent and is reminiscent of a pie baking in the oven while the leaves are changing colors.

Submitted by: Cole Levy

Serve in a small rocks glass

Ingredients:
- 2 ounces Butchers Cut Bourbon
- 3 candied orange segments
- 1 ounce Licor 43
- ¾ ounce ginger beer
- ½ ounce lime juice

Preparation:
1. Muddle candied orange segments in small tin.
2. Starting with citrus and ending with bourbon, add remaining ingredients (reverse of the order above).
3. Shake cocktail over ice until tin freezes (about 30 seconds).
4. Double strain into a chilled small rocks glass.

Orange You Glad

by Detroit City Distillery

Distillery 291

1647 South Tejon Street
Colorado Springs, Colorado 80905
(719) 323-8010

distillery291.com
info@distillery291.com

Established
2011

Leadership
Distillery 291 was founded by former fashion and beauty photographer, Michael Myers and is owned by a small group of proprietors.

291 Bourbon Lemonade

The 291 Bourbon Lemonade is the ideal summer cocktail. It's simple to make and packs a punch.

Submitted by: Distillery 291

Serve in an 8 ounce Collins glass

Ingredients:
- 1 ounce fresh squeezed lemon juice
- 1 ounce raw sugar simple syrup
- 2 ounces 291 Colorado Bourbon Whiskey

Preparation:
1. Place all ingredients in cocktail shaker with ice.
2. Shake well.
3. Serve over ice in a Collins glass.

DogMaster Distillery

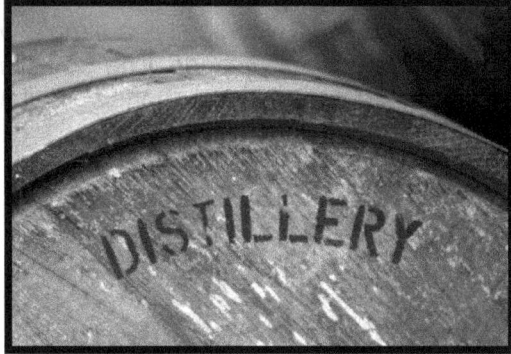

210 St. James Street, Suite D
Columbia, Missouri 65201
(573) 825-6066

dogmasterdistillery.com
dogmaster@dogmasterdistillery.com

Established
2014

Leadership
Van and Lisa Driskel Hawxby
Dan and Stephanie Batliner

Bourbon Cherry Smash

Using fruit preserves in a cocktail is a simple way to introduce intense flavors in your beverages. The Bourbon Cherry Smash is an easy to construct, strong bourbon cocktail with big flavor.

Submitted by: Van Hawxby (cocktail creator)

Serve in a martini glass

Ingredients:
- 2 ounces bourbon
- 2 tablespoons tart cherry preserves
- Splash of orange juice
- Splash of club soda
- Orange wedge

Preparation:
1. Combine all ingredients, other than orange wedge, with ice in a cocktail shaker and shake vigorously.
2. Strain into a chilled martini glass.
3. Garnish with an orange wedge.

Bourbon Cherry Smash

by DogMaster Distillery

Dry Diggings Distillery

5050 Robert J Mathews Parkway
El Dorado Hills, California 95762
(916) 542-1700

drydiggingsdistillery.com
chris.drydiggings@gmail.com

Established
2008

Leadership
Cris Steller & Gordon Helm

The leadership also owns Amador Distillery / amadordistillery.com

DRY DIGGINGS
DISTILLERY

Briar Patch

For some, the thought of barrel proof bourbon seems as abrasive as a walk through a briar patch. This well-balanced cocktail inspired by the classic Boulevardier makes the whole trip enjoyable for all. The lively aromatics from the lavender and thyme turn your cocktail into a journey. The blackberry in framboise is the perfect sweet reward when you get to the finish line. The Briar Patch includes all Califonia spirits, local herbs and blackberries in framboise from a local craftsmen.

Submitted by: Charles Roehr of Magpie Cafe Sacramento

Serve in a bucket glass

Ingredients:
- 1 ¼ ounces Engine 49 120 proof bourbon
- ¾ ounce St. George Bruto Americano
- ¼ ounce St. George Raspberry Liqueur
- ¾ ounce Gallo Dry Vermouth
- Dried lavender flower
- Thyme sprig
- One blackberry in framboise from Jolly Trading Co.

Preparation:
1. Pour all ingredients into a mixing glass.
2. Add ice and stir.
3. Double strain into a bucket glass with a single large ice cube.
4. Garnish with dried lavender flower and thyme sprig for aromatics.
5. On a pick, garnish with blackberry.

Briar Patch

by Dry Diggings Distillery

FEW Spirits

918 Chicago Avenue
Evanston, Illinois 60202
(847) 920-8628

fewspirits.com
info@fewspirits.com

Established
2011

Leadership
Paul Hletko, Owner

That 773 Though

The That 773 Though is a bourbon-forward aperitif that's simultaneously boozy and light and sweet. The drink was created in honor of the distillery's fifth birthday by Tonia Guffey at Dram in Brooklyn. The name comes from one of Chicago's area codes.

Submitted by: Tonia Guffey, Dram in Brooklyn

Serve in a cocktail glass

Ingredients:
- 1 ounce FEW Bourbon Whiskey
- ¾ ounce Aperol
- ¾ ounce St. Germain
- ¾ ounce lemon juice
- Lemon twist

Preparation:
1. Add all the ingredients to a shaker and fill with ice.
2. Shake, and strain into a cocktail glass.
3. Garnish with a lemon twist.

That 773 Though

by Few Spirits

Grand Traverse Distillery

781 Industrial Circle, Suite 5
Traverse City, Michigan 49686
(231) 947-8635

grandtraversedistillery.com
info@grandtraversedistillery.com

Established
2005

Leadership
Kent Rabish, President

Smoked Honey Whiskey Sour

We smoke local honey in house, and this cocktail has been a well-loved classic and staple for our downtown Traverse City tasting room!

Submitted by: Grand Traverse Distillery

Serve in a coupe

Ingredients:
- 2 ounces bourbon
- 1 ounce smoked honey
- 1 ounce lemon juice
- ½ ounce egg white
- 2 dashes of bitters

Preparation:
1. In a shaker, add all ingredients listed above.
2. Dry shake the mixture (no ice) for 15 seconds.
3. Add ice to the shaker and shake for an additional 10 seconds.
4. Strain the cocktail into a chilled coupe glass, and garnish with an orange and a cherry spear.

Smoked Honey Whiskey Sour

by Grand Traverse Distillery

Glacier Distilling Company

10237 Highway 2 E.
Coram, Montana 59913
(406) 387-9887

glacierdistilling.com

Established
2010

Leadership
Nic Lee, Founder

Firebrand Pass

Perfect for the holidays, many say the Firebrand Pass tastes like "Christmas in your mouth."

Submitted by: Glacier Distilling Company

Serve in a copper mug

Ingredients:
- 1 ½ ounces Fireweed Bourbon
- 1 ounce spiced cranberry simple syrup*
- 1 ounce citrus mix**
- Ice
- Ginger beer
- Rosemary
- Fresh cranberries

Preparation:
1. Add ice to copper mug.
2. Add bourbon, cranberry simple syrup and citrus mix.
3. Top with ginger beer.
4. Garnish with spanked rosemary (spanked to release the flavor) and a few fresh cranberries for a pop of color.

*Prep for Spiced Cranberry Simple Syrup: In a pot add 1 cup packed brown sugar, 1 cup raw sugar, 1 cup cranberries (fresh or frozen), 1 ½ cups water, 5 cinnamon sticks, and 2 star anise. Simmer ingredients for about 20 minutes. Strain ingredients and cool simple for use.

**Prep for Citrus Mix: In a container, combine two parts orange juice to one part each of lime and lemon concentrate.

Honeoye Falls Distillery

168 West Main Street
Honeoye Falls, NY 14472
(585) 624-1700

hfdistillery.com
info@hfdistillery.com

Established
2015

Leadership
Teal Schlegel, Head Distiller/Co-Founder
Scott Stanton -CEO/Co-Founder

NY Sour

Submitted by: Honeoye Falls Distillery

or
Serve in a rocks glass or vintage coupe

Ingredients:
- 1 ½ ounces Red Saw Bourbon
- ¾ ounce simple syrup
- ¼ ounce lemon juice
- ¼ ounce lime juice
- Red or pluot wine

Preparation:
1. In a shaker, combine all ingredients, except wine, with a large chunk of ice.
2. Shake quickly and vigorously, then strain into glass.
3. Top with a wine float.

NY Sour

by Honeoye Falls Distillery

Hotel Tango Artisan Distillery

702 Virginia Avenue
Indianapolis, Indiana 46203

hoteltangowhiskey.com

Established
2014

Leadership
Travis Barnes, Founder

Hotel Tango is proud to be the first disabled veteran-owned distillery in the United States and the first artisan distillery in Indianapolis since Prohibition.

In The Weeds

"In The Weeds" is Hotel Tango's springtime take on a classic Old Fashioned. As an artisan distillery, they hand-make all ingredients in-house, including the lemongrass simple syrup and tart cherry-saffron bitters. The first and foremost goal of their craft cocktails is to showcase their artisan spirits, but they note they can't help but to elevate the experience with creative flavors from infusions and more.

Submitted by: Hotel Tango Artisan Distillery

Serve in a rocks glass

Ingredients:
- 2 ounces Bravo Bourbon
- ½ ounce lemongrass simple syrup
- 2-3 drops tart cherry-saffron bitters
- Lemon swath for garnish

Preparation:
1. Add ingredients to a single rocks glass and stir.
2. Serve on a large cube, garnished with a lemon swath.

In The Weeds

by Hotel Tango Artisan Distillery

Indian Creek Distillery

7095 Staley Road
New Carlisle, Ohio 45344
(937) 846-1443

staleymillfarmanddistillery.com
indiancreekwhiskey@gmail.com

Established
1820 (originally) and opened again in 2012

Leadership
Melissa and Joe Duer

Witchy Whiskey Woman

This cocktail is a liquid incantation, based on healing spell. Cinnamon was once used to treat infections and properties in nutmeg were used to treat tooth pain. Star Anise is an anti-fungal and was a known cure for arthritis. Tobacco once called the Holy Herb, the leaves were burned to disinfect and ward off disease.

Well balanced, with a taste of everything in every sip, spicy, sweet, citrus, bitter and earthy. This libation is full of interest and flavor. Excellent for sipping by a summer evening bonfire or cozied up next to the fireplace in the winter.

Submitted by: Sailor Retro

Serve in a coupe

Ingredients:
- 2 ounces Andy's Old No. 5 Bourbon
- 1 teaspoon cinnamon spice syrup*
- 1 teaspoon falernum syrup**
- 1 pinch of nutmeg
- 1 pinch of cinnamon
- 4 shakes of Medicine Man Tobacco Bitters
- 1 teaspoon fernet branca
- 1 teaspoon absinthe
- 1 large lemon peel
- Lighter

Preparation:
1. In a cocktail shaker, combine ice and all ingredients (except for the lemon peel, cinnamon and lighter).

Preparation (continued):

2. Shake well until the outside of the cocktail shaker is cold to the touch.
3. Strain into a coupe glass with a fine cocktail strainer.
4. Garnish with a large lemon peel.
5. Heat the outside of the lemon peel with a lighter to open the pores in the peel, this will allow the oil to incorporate into the cocktail.
6. Sprinkle a small pinch of cinnamon onto the top of the cocktail and enjoy.

*Cinnamon Spice Syrup:

Add one cup of water to a medium pot. Add 1 tablespoon cinnamon, 1 star of anise, 1 tablespoon nutmeg, 1 vanilla bean, 1 tablespoon ginger and 1 cup of sugar. Boil for 20-30 minutes on medium covered until all of the sugar is dissolved. Allow the mixture to cool, strain into a glass bottle or jar with a coffee filter. Store in the refrigerator.

**Falernum Syrup:

Fee Brothers, Tipplemans and John D. Taylor's are some recommended brands.

Kings County Distillery

299 Sands Street
Brooklyn Navy Yard
Brooklyn, New York 11205
(347) 689-4211

kingscountydistillery.com
info@kingscountydistillery.com

Established
2010

Leadership
Colin Spoelman and David Haskell, Co-Founders

KINGS COUNTY DISTILLERY
NEW YORK CITY'S OLDEST WHISKEY DISTILLERY

Kings County Mint Julep

Mint Juleps are properly made with mint-infused simple syrup. Throughout most of American history, drinks were made using a lot of sugar—it seems that old recipes were designed for palates that weren't already inundated with high-fructose corn syrup. I tend to suggest adjusting the recipe to taste, and less sugar means you have more opportunity to taste the bourbon, which for the bourbon fan is a good thing.

Submitted by: Colin Spoelman

Serve in a silver or pewter julep cup

Ingredients:
- 2 ounces bourbon
- 1 ounce mint simple syrup*
- 3-4 mint leaves

Preparation:
1. Fill julep cup with crushed ice.
2. Add bourbon, mint syrup, and top with a rounded scoop of crushed ice.
3. Garnish with a mint sprig.

*Mint Syrup:
Use one part sugar to one part water and heat on low heat with muddled mint sprigs. Heat until the sugar dissolves and then take off heat and let cool before storing in the refrigerator.

Kings County Mint Julep

by Kings County Distillery

Liberty Call Distilling

2739 Via Orange Way #110
Spring Valley California 91978
(619) 630-1240

libertycalldistilling.com
info@libertycalldistilling.com

Established
2013

Leadership
Bill Rogers, Founder
Steve Grella, Distiller
Addison Poth, Brewer

Blackberry Julep

The Blackberry Julep is a refreshing summertime drink using fresh, local blackberries that really enhance the drink's flavor.

Submitted by: Albert Allison

Serve in a julep cup

Ingredients:

- 3 ounces Blue Ridge 4-Grain Whiskey
- ½ ounce blackberry simple syrup
- 12 mint leaves
- Sliced blackberry

Preparation:

1. Muddle mint leaves and simple syrup in bottom of julep glass.
2. Add crushed ice, pour bourbon on top then garnish with sliced blackberry and serve.

Liberty Pole Spirits

68 West Maiden Street
Washington, Pennsylvania 15301
(724) 503-4014

libertypolespirits.com
info@mingocreekcraftdistillers.com

Established
2016

Leadership
The Hough family (Jim, Ellen, Rob, and Kevin)

Lemon Basilsmith

This recipe was inspired when Ellen Hough was asked to come up with a cocktail using our bourbon to pair with an Italian-themed buffet they were hosting at the distillery. Since basil is such a perfect complement to Italian food, she came up with this light and refreshing cocktail using the fresh basil they grow in their herb garden behind the distillery.

Submitted by: Ellen Hough

Serve in a goblet

Ingredients:
- 2 ounces Liberty Pole Spirits Bourbon
- 2 ounces basil simple syrup
- 2 ounces fresh squeezed lemon juice

Preparation:
1. Combine ingredients in cocktail shaker with ice and shake vigorously.
2. Fill goblet glass with fresh ice and strain into glass.
3. Garnish with fresh basil sprig.

Lemon Basilsmith

by Liberty Pole Distillers

Mad River Distillers

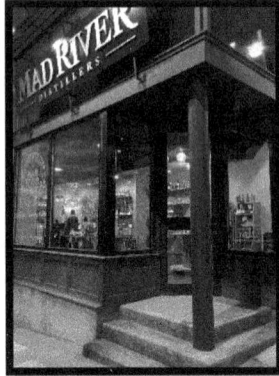

137 St. Paul Street
Burlington, Vermont 05401
(802) 489-5501

madriverdistillers.com
info@madriverdistillers.com

Leadership
Mimi Buttenheim, President
Alex Hilton, Distiller/GM
Neil Goldberg, Retail Manager

Maple Bourbon Sour

When Mad River first opened its tasting room the cocktail menu had five offerings, all focused on pairing its Vermont made spirits with other unique and delicious Vermont made products. The maple syrup is aged in former bourbon barrels. As a result, the bourbon and maple syrup come together like old friends in this Vermont twist on a classic.

Submitted by: Neil Goldberg

Serve in a double old fashioned glass

Ingredients:
- 2 ounces Mad River Bourbon
- 1 ounce fresh lemon juice
- 1 ounce Al Wood's Vermont Bourbon Barrel Aged Maple Syrup
- 3 dashes Angostura Bitters
- Lemon twist

Preparation:
1. In shaker with ice, add the first three ingredients.
2. Shake hard and strain over large ice cube in double old fashioned glass.
3. Express oil from lemon by twisting over the top of the drink, rub the rim of the glass, and throw the peel away.
4. Add 3 dashes of Angostura bitters.

Note: If possible add bitters to an atomizer and spray bitters across the top for a more even dispersion.

Motor City Gas Whiskey Distillery

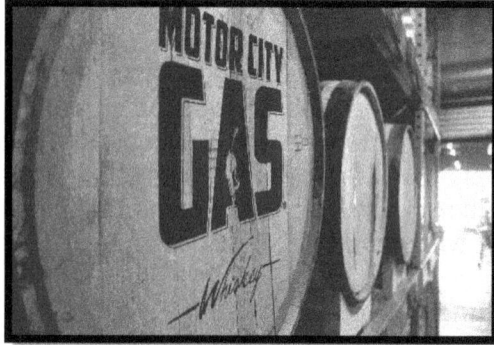

325 East Fourth Street
Royal Oak, Michigan 48067
(248) 599-1427

motorcitygas.com
motorcitygas@gmail.com

Established
2015

Leadership
Rich Lockwood, Owner and Master Distiller

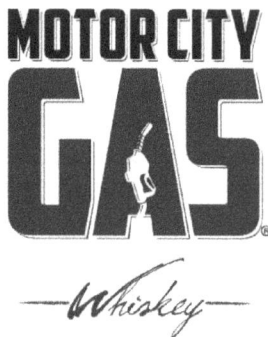

Apple Sauced

This cocktail is made from two spirits that are made from grain to glass at Motor City Gas. "Belly Up Bourbon" is a high rye bourbon that is finished in a Caribbean rum barrel and "Apple Sauce" is a whiskey moonshine blended with Michigan apple cider, infused in a house spice blend and then barrel aged in our own rye whiskey barrels. The two create complexity and balance without the help of juices, biters, vinegars, or other flavorings commonly used in today's craft cocktail scene.

Submitted by: Motor City Gas

Serve in a rocks glass

Ingredients:
- 1 ½ ounces rum barrel finished Belly Up Bourbon
- 1 ½ ounces apple sauce moonshine
- Cinnamon stick
- Red apple slices
- 1 cinnamon stick

Preparation:
1. Combine all ingredients in a rocks glass with ice.
2. Stir.
3. Garnish with cinnamon stick and red apple slices.

Apple Sauced

by Motor City Gas Whiskey Distillery

Myer Farm Distillers

7350 State Route 89
Ovid, New York, 14521
(607) 532-4800

myerfarmdistillers.com
joe@myerfarmdistillers.com

Established
2012

Leadership
Joseph Myer, President and Master Distiller
John Myer, Vice President and Farmer

Summer's Rays

Located in an area with a lot of black walnut trees, a distinguished bitters-maker, and several cideries, this cocktail from Myer Farm Distillers was created to represent the region. There's a lot going on in the drink, but the ingredients configure well together.

Submitted by: Myer Farm Distillers (Nikki Reese, Tasting Room Manager and Marketing Assistant)

Serve in a rocks glass

Ingredients:

- 2 ounces John Myer Bourbon
- Fresh chocolate mint leaf
- ¼ ounce maple syrup
- 5-6 dashes of Fee Brothers Black Walnut Bitters
- Sparkling cider
- Orange slice

Preparation:

1. In a mixing glass, muddle a chocolate mint leaf with maple syrup.
2. Fill glass with ice and pour in and add bourbon and black walnut bitters.
3. Shake well and pour into a rocks glass, top with sparkling cider.
4. Garnish with a slice of orange.

Summer's Rays

by Myer Farm Distillers

OOLA Distillery

1314 East Union Street
Seattle, Washington 98122
(206) 709-7907

ooladistillery.com
info@ooladistillery.com

Established
2010

Leadership
Kirby Kallas-Lewis

Maximiliano aka King Max

One of the all-time favorite classic cocktails of OOLA Distillery distiller John Fausz is the Boulevardier: a richly balanced variation on the Negroni that swaps out Bourbon for Gin. This provides a nice interplay between the rich vanilla and caramel notes in the whiskey, similar spicy oxidative flavors in sweet vermouth, all capped by a bright, bitter orange from the Campari. John notes his take on this classic is, "thoroughly European, yet with New World pretense and a fiery end."

Submitted by: John Fausz, Distiller and Brand Ambassador

Serve in a vintage coupe

Ingredients:
- 2 ounces Waitsburg Bourbon Whiskey
- ½ ounce sweet vermouth
- ½ ounce Campari
- Splash of Cointreau
- Dash of Scrappy's Firewater Tincture
- Orange twist

Preparation:
1. Place all ingredients in a shaker with ice.
2. Shake.
3. Strain into a coupe.
4. Garnish with an orange twist.

Maximiliano aka King Max

by OOLA Distillery

Painted Stave Distilling

106 West Commerce Street
Smyrna, Delaware 19977
(302) 653-6834

paintedstave.com
hello@paintedstave.com

Established
2011

Leadership
Ron Gomes and Mike Rasmussen, Co-Owners

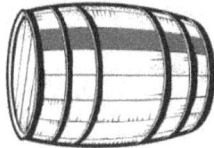

Whiskey Smash

Submitted by: Painted Stave Distilling

Serve in a rocks glass

Ingredients:
- 5-7 mint leaves (garden fresh)
- 2 ounces Diamond State Straight Bourbon Whiskey
- ¾ ounce simple syrup
- ¾ ounce fresh squeezed lemon juice
- 1 lemon wheel (for garnish)

Preparation:
1. Put 5-7 mint leaves into a shaker and add ice (filling 1/2 of the shaker).
2. Add bourbon, simple syrup and lemon juice.
3. Shake well (until the outside of tumbler is frosty).
4. Pour everything into a rocks glass and garnish with a lemon wheel.

Whiskey Smash

by Painted Stave Distilling

Rabbit Hole Distilling

711 East Jefferson Street
Louisville, Kentucky 40202
(502) 561-2000

rabbitholedistilling.com
info@rabbitholedistilling.com

Established
2012

Leadership
Kaveh Zamanian

Saint Boulevardier

Rabbit Hole is built upon tradition with a modern approach. This cocktail is based on that idea that the classic Boulevardier gets an updated touch with the addition of beautifully floral St. Germain.

Submitted by: Ryan Easterly, Brand Manager

Serve in a rocks glass

Ingredients:
- 1 ounce Rabbit Hole Rye
- 1 ounce Carpano Antica Vermouth
- ¾ ounce Campari
- ¼ ounce St. Germain

Preparation:
1. Add all ingredients to a mixing glass.
2. Stir well.
3. Strain over a large ice cube in a rocks glass.
4. Garnish with a zest of orange.

Ranger Creek Brewing and Distilling

4834 Whirlwind Drive
San Antonio, Texas 78217
(210) 775-2099

drinkrangercreek.com
info@drinkrangercreek.com

Established
2010

Leadership
Mark McDavid, TJ Miller and Dennis Rylander, Co-Founders

Ranger Creek Tea Tapper

It's hot in Texas, so the Ranger Creek team uses their .36 Texas Bourbon in a refreshing cocktail that incorporates sweet tea. The key is to not use too much tea so that the bourbon still shines. This is a great recipe to batch up in a pitcher and enjoy by the pool on a hot day.

Submitted by: Dani Call

Serve in an old fashioned glass

Ingredients:
- 2 ounces sweet tea
- ¾ ounce pomegranate juice
- 1 ½ ounces Ranger Creek .36 Texas Bourbon
- 1 slice lemon
- 1 slice orange

Preparation:
1. Fill an old fashioned glass ¾ of the way to the top with ice. Mix liquids in and stir.
2. Rim glass with lemon.
3. Garnish with orange slice and serve.

Ranger Creek Tea Tapper

by Ranger Creek Brewing and Distillery

Red Eagle Distillery

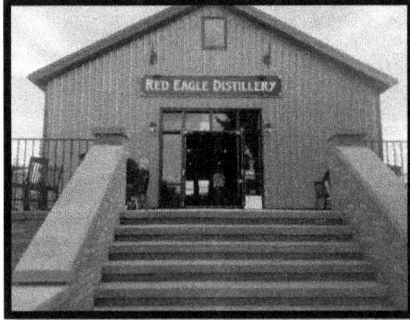

6202 South River Road
Geneva, Ohio 44041
(440) 466-6604

redeaglespirits.com

Established
2012

Leadership
Gene and Heather Sigel

The Peachy Keen

Submitted by: Red Eagle Distillery

Serve in a stemmed wine glass

Ingredients:
- 1 ½ ounces Red Eagle Bourbon
- ½ ounce basil honey simple syrup
- 2 ounces peach nectar
- 2 ounces prosecco or sparkling wine
- Lemon wheel
- Fresh basil

Preparation:
1. In a glass, add bourbon, basil honey simple syrup and peach nectar.
2. Stir.
3. Top off with prosecco or sparkling wine.
4. Garnish with lemon wheel and fresh basil.

The Peachy Keen

by Red Eagle Distillery

Reservoir Distillery

1800 A Summit Avenue
Richmond, Virginia 23230
(804) 912-2621

reservoirdistillery.com
info@reservoirdistillery.com

Established
2008

Leadership
Dave Cuttino & Jay Carpenter, Co-Owner

RESERVOIR
DISTILLERY
RICHMOND, VIRGINIA

Reservoir Bourbon Bloody

Reservoir Bourbon Bloody came out of a collaboration with Beth Dixon of Pasture Restaurant. The goal was to highlight the creative use of one of the used 5-gallon bourbon barrels to age the smokey and spicy D'Lish Sauce, made by James Beard Semifinalist Sydney Meers of Stove Restaurant in Portsmouth, Virginia. The addition of Reservoir Bourbon, and a few other ingredients, yields a wickedly delicious twist on this classic cocktail.

Submitted by: Reservoir Distillery, LLC

Serve in a highball glass

Ingredients:
- 1 ½ ounces Reservoir Bourbon
- 4 ½ ounces Bloody Mix*
- Lime wedge

Preparation:
1. Fill glass with ice.
2. Add bourbon and Bloody Mix.
3. Stir to combine.
4. Add lime wedge for garnish.

*Bloody Mix
Ingredients:
- ¾ cup tomato juice
- ¾ cup V8
- 2 teaspoons horseradish
- ¾ teaspoon celery salt
- ¼ teaspoon black pepper

Bloody Mix (continued)
- 3 tablespoons + ½ teaspoon lemon juice
- 3 tablespoons + ½ teaspoon lime juice
- ¼ cup Worcestershire
- 2 tablespoons D'lish
- 1 tablespoon Not Hot Sauce

Preparation:
1. Combine all ingredients and mix well.

St. Augustine Distillery Company

Historic Ice Plant
112 Riberia Street
St. Augustine, Florida 32084
(904) 825-4962

staugustinedistillery.com
info@staugustinedistillery.com

Established
2011

Leadership
Philip McDaniel, CEO / Co-Founder
Mike Diaz, CFO / Co-Founder

Old City, Old Fashioned

St. Augustine's bourbon cocktail involves a partnership with Joe and Maryelana at Bittermilk (Charleston, South Carolina). Working with the team at Bittermilk, they developed a proprietary, private label cocktail mixer. Bittermilk repurposes St. Augustine's used bourbon barrels to age this Old Fashioned cocktail mixer, which contains Florida Cane Juice, Molasses, Orange Peel, Spices, Gentian Root and Cinchona Bark. It's a unique partnership that makes for one of the most delicious, easy-to-make Old Fashioned cocktails.

Submitted by: St. Augustine Distillery

Serve in a 6-10 ounce rocks glass

Ingredients:
- 2 ounces St. Augustine Double Cask Bourbon
- ½ ounce St. Augustine Old Fashioned Mix
- Wafer thin, orange peel about 1" in size

Preparation:
1. In a rocks glass, fill with large format, slow melt ice cubes.
2. Add Old Fashioned Mix followed by Double Cask Bourbon.
3. Stir until glass is cold to the touch.
4. Fold or twist orange peel until oils are released.
5. Rub peel around rim and brush sides of glass to impart orange fragrance.

Old City, Old Fashioned

by St. Augustine Distillery

San Diego Distillery

2766 Via Orange Way Suite H
Spring Valley, California 91978
(619) 361-1525

sddistillery.com
trent@sddistillery.com

Established
2014

Leadership
Trent and Maria Tilton

Chocolate Old Fashioned

This cocktail is just based upon some of our favorite things of San Diego Distillery owners Trent and Maria Tilton: an Old Fashioned cocktail and chocolate. It is a tasting room favorite.

Submitted by: Trent Tilton

Serve in a rocks glass

Ingredients:
- 1 ½ ounces San Diego Distillery Bourbon
- ½ ounce Crème de Cocoa
- 4-6 dashes of chocolate bitters
- Cherry
- Orange zest

Preparation:
1. Add bourbon, Crème de Cocoa and bitters in a rocks glass with ice.
2. Stir.
3. Add cherry and orange zest for garnish.

Chocolate Old Fashioned

by San Diego Distillery

Silverback Distillery

9374 Rockfish Valley Highway
Afton, Virginia 22920
(540) 456-7070

sbdistillery.com
christine@sbdistillery.com

Established
2013

Leadership
Christine and Denver Riggleman

The Smoked Old Fashioned

The Smoked Old Fashioned cocktail is such a fun drink! It may be a little difficult to get your hands on an oak stave, but it's absolutely worth it. The smokiness of the glass, paired with the smooth bourbon and sweet maple syrup, makes for an amazingly complex and tasty drink.

Submitted by: Lauren Riggleman

Serve in a rocks glass

Ingredients:
- 2 ounces Blackback Bourbon
- 1 ounce Virginia maple syrup
- ½ ounce Angostura Bitters
- Orange wheel
- Cherry

Preparation:
1. Take a white oak stave and set it on fire.
2. Place your rocks glass upside down over the flame so that it can capture the smoke.
3. Turn over the glass, and fill with one large ice cube, bourbon, maple syrup and bitters.
4. Garnish with orange wheel and cherry.

The Smoked Old Fashioned

by Silverback Distillery

StiLL 630 Distillery

1000 South Fourth Street
St. Louis, Missouri 63104

still630.com
david@still630.com

Established
2011

Leadership
David Weglarz
Jim Schultz
Dyke Minix
Ben Pippenger

Wally's Breakfast

Submitted by: Andrew Spaugh (creator)

Serve in a rocks glass

Ingredients:
- 1 ½ ounces Monon Bell Bourbon
- 1 ounce dry vermouth
- 1 ½ ounces espresso/dark roast
- 3 dashes of orange bitters
- 1 sugar cube
- 2 slices of orange
- 1 cinnamon stick

Preparation:
1. Muddle sugar cube, 1 orange slice and orange bitters in a shaker.
2. Add in bourbon, espresso and vermouth, and shake.
3. Strain and serve over ice.
4. Garnish with other orange slice and cinnamon stick.

Wally's Breakfast

by StiLL 630 Distillery

Striped Pig Distillery

2225 Old School Drive
Charleston, South Carolina 29466
(843) 276-3201

stripedpigdistillery.com
info@stripedpigdistillery.com

Established
2013

Leadership
Todd Weiss
James Craig
Johnny Pieper

Chucktown Sunrise

At the Striped Pig, they like to keep things simple. They have found that when a drink recipe is too complicated, folks won't make it. Drinking should be relaxing and enjoyable, not a chore. That's why they offer people simple, tasting cocktails.

Submitted by: Striped Pig Distillery and **Southern Living Magazine**

Serve in a pint glass

Ingredients:
- 2 tablespoons bourbon
- 1 ½ teaspoons fresh lime juice
- Ice
- 6 tablespoons ginger beer
- ¼ teaspoon grenadine
- Fresh lime slices or wedges for garnish

Preparation:
1. Combine bourbon and fresh lime juice in a cocktail shaker.
2. Fill with ice.
3. Cover with lid, and shake vigorously until thoroughly chilled (about 30 seconds).
4. Strain into a 10-oz. glass filled with ice.
5. Top with your favorite ginger ale or ginger beer.
6. Drizzle with grenadine.
7. Garnish with fresh lime slices or wedges.

Chucktown Sunrise

by Striped Pig Distillery

Stumpy's Spirits Distillery

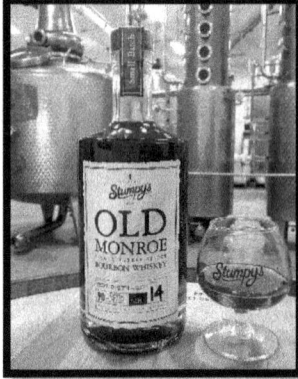

1727 Centerville Road
Columbia, Illinois 62236
(618) 281-7733

stumpysspirits.com
contact@stumpysspirits.com

Established
2014

Leadership
Adam and Laura Stumpf, Co-Owners

Old Monroe Peach Lemonade

Fresh peaches are a summertime staple in our community. This cocktail features two local favorites, Old Monroe Bourbon and fresh, ripe peaches. This perfect blend of sweet, tart and fruity flavors is best enjoyed surrounded by family and friends!

Submitted by: Laura Stumpf

Serve in an old fashioned glass

Ingredients:
- ½ ripe peach, diced
- 1 ½ ounces Old Monroe Bourbon
- 4 ounces fresh lemonade
- Ice
- Garnish with fresh lemon slice and a peach wedge

Preparation:
1. Muddle diced peaches in old fashioned glass.
2. Fill glass with ice.
3. Pour Old Monroe Bourbon over ice.
4. Top with lemonade.
5. Stir, garnish, & enjoy!

Old Monroe Peach Lemonade

by Stumpy's Spirits Distillery

Sugar House Distillery

2212 South West Temple, Unit #14
Salt Lake City, Utah 84115
(801) 726-0403

sugarhousedistillery.net
info@sugarhousedistillery.net

Established
2013

Leadership
James Fowler, Owner

Mountain West Manhattan

Although you'll usually find the crew at Sugar House Distillery sipping their bourbon neat, after a first-tracks morning skiing Utah's legendarily deep powder, they do love good cocktail. Especially when it's a spin on a classic, like this spicy, sweet and particularly sassy interpretation of a Black Manhattan. It's mixed up with ingredients like traditional Averna, a touch of guajillo-honey syrup (that'd be a nod to the Beehive State's abundance of high-desert farmsteads) and snappy local-made sarsaparilla-sassafras bitters. A true grain-to-glass operation, the SHD distillers source all of the grains for their dynamic small-batch bourbon within a 120-mile radius directly from farmers, ferment with house-cultivated yeast strains and bottle with the purest mountain water.

Submitted by: Darby Doyle (*abourbongal.com*)

Serve in a coupe glass

Ingredients:
- 2 ounces Sugar House Distillery Bourbon
- ¾ ounce Averna Amaro
- ¼ ounce spiced guajillo-honey syrup*
- 4 dashes Honest John Bitters Co. Sarsaparilla Bitters

Preparation:
1. Add all ingredients into a stirring glass with ice.
2. Stir until well chilled; strain into a chilled coupe glass.
3. Express the oil from a generous strip of orange zest over the top of the drink and rub the rim and stem of glass with orange zest, then discard zest.

Preparation (continued):
   4.   Garnish with a brandied cherry.

*Spiced Guajillo Honey Syrup:
In a small saucepan, bring to a simmer one guajillo chili pod, ½ cup raw honey and ¾ cup water. Simmer until honey is completely dissolved and liquid takes on a slight orange hue from the chili (about 5-7 minutes). Remove from heat; let sit at room temperature for about 4-5 hours. Strain to remove solids, pour into a re-sealable glass jar, and refrigerate until use. Makes about ¾ cup syrup.

Mountain West Manhattan

by Sugar House Distillery

Syntax Spirits Distillery and Cocktail Bar

625 3rd Street, Unit C
Greeley, Colorado 80631
(Note: In 2018, Syntax Spirits will be moving to 700 6th Street,
Greeley, Colorado, an old grain elevator which is pictured above)
(970) 352-5466

syntaxspirits.com
info@syntaxspirits.com

Established
2010

Leadership
Heather Bean, CEO & Jeff Copeland, CFO

The Jack(al)

This drink is named after Captain Jack, our distillery "kitten" that plays sidekick to our OG distillery cat, Gustav. Gustav is the undisputed king of rodent-control and guest-charming, sometimes both at the same time. Gus is working very hard to train C. Jack up in his image, and we're all for it. As such, this drink is a little bit sweet, a little bit orange, and a fair chunk naughty.

Submitted by: Syntax!

Serve in a stemmed wine glass

Ingredients:
- 4 ounces Syntax Spirits Bourbon
- 2 ounces Averna Amaro Siciliano
- Several splashes Peychaud or Angostura Orange Bitters
- 1 tablespoon fresh orange juice

Preparation:
1. Combine all ingredients in a mixing glass and stir with ice.
2. Strain into a stemmed wine glass.
3. Garnish with twist of orange peel.

The Jack(al)

by Syntax Spirits

Taconic Distillery

179 Bowen Road
Stanfordville, New York 12581
(845) 393-4583

taconicdistillery.com
cac@taconicdistillery.com

Established
2013

Leadership
Paul and Carol Ann Coughlin

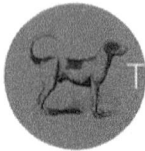

Copper's Tail

Copper's Tail is named for our American Foxhound, Copper, who is featured on our logo and all of our product labels. Copper (the foxhound) is named for the color of our continuous column still, as well as the rich color of our bourbon.

Submitted by: Taconic Distillery

Serve in a chilled rocks glass

Ingredients:
- 2 ounces Taconic Bourbon
- 1 ounce Taconic Maple Syrup
- 1 ounce orange liqueur (Grand Marnier or Cointreau)
- 1 clementine, juiced
- ½ lemon, juiced

Preparation:
1. Fill shaker halfway with ice.
2. Pour in bourbon, maple syrup, orange liqueur, clementine juice and lemon juice.
3. Shake well.
4. Strain into a chilled rocks glass.
5. Garnish with orange/clementine slice.

Copper's Tail

by Taconic Distillery

Timber Creek Distillery

6538 Lake Ella Road
Crestview, Florida 32539
(408) 439-0973

timbercreekdistillery.com
camden@timbercreekdistillery.com

Established
2014

Leadership
Camden Ford & Aaron Barnes

QUALITY DISTILLING BY LOCAL ARTISANS
TIMBER
CREEK
DISTILLERY

Blackberry Rye Old Fashioned

Our black rye is a one-of-a-kind rye whiskey made from 100% Florida 401 Black Rye; a strain that grows only in Florida. It contains a uniquely bold flavor unlike any other rye.

Submitted by: Timber Creek Distillery

Serve in a chilled rocks glass

Ingredients:
- 1 ½ ounces Timber Creek Black Rye Whiskey
- 2 dashes Angostura bitter
- 1 sugar cube
- 1 bar spoon water
- 2 blackberries
- Orange twist (optional)

Preparation:
1. Muddle the sugar cube, bitters, and blackberries with water at the bottom of a chilled glass.
2. Add rye and one large ice cube.
3. Stir for about 30 seconds.
4. Serve with an orange twist.

Tom's Foolery Distillery

17520 Rapids Road
Troy Township, Ohio 44021

tomsfoolery.com
tom@tomsfoolery.com or lianne@tomsfoolery.com

Established
2008

Leadership
Tom and Lianne Herbruck

An Apple A Day

Apples are a staple crop in Ohio and many artisans use them to their advantage. They are the only ingredient in our Applejack and many locals make delicious apple butter that works perfectly as a slightly sweet and sour component to shaken cocktails. The two combined equate to a luscious libation with great viscosity. Balanced with our bourbon and bitterness from Averna Amaro, this cocktail is a crowd pleaser.

Submitted by: Lorilei Bailey, mixologist extraordinaire for Tom's Foolery Distillery

Serve in a rocks glass

Ingredients:
- 1 ½ ounce Tom's Foolery Bourbon
- ½ ounce Tom's Foolery Applejack
- ½ ounce Averna Amaro
- 2 tablespoons Apple Butter
- 3 dashes Angostura Bitters
- 1 orange peel
- 1 Luxardo cherry

Preparation:
1. Combine all ingredients except the orange peel and cherry into a mixing tin.
2. Add ice, then shake until well chilled.
3. Strain into a rocks glass over fresh ice.
4. Garnish with an orange peel and Luxardo cherry.

An Apple A Day

by Tom's Foolery Distillery

Town Branch Distillery

401 Cross Street
Lexington, Kentucky 40508

townbranchbourbon.com
kentuckyale@alltech.com

Established
2011

Leadership
Mark Coffman, Master Distiller

Town Branch
Distillery
EST. 2012

Bourbon Ball Martini

Created for a cocktail competition in Lexington, KY, the Bourbon Ball Martini came out as the clear winner for dessert cocktails. This cocktail also went on to win the cocktail contest at the Kentucky Bourbon Festival in 2016.

Submitted by: Mark O'Shea

Serve in a martini glass

Ingredients:
- 1 Part Town Branch Bourbon
- 1 Part Bluegrass Sundown Bourbon Coffee Liqueur
- 1 Part Simple Syrup
- 1 Part Crème de Cocoa
- Bailey's Irish Cream

Preparation:
1. Mix the Town Branch Bourbon, Bluegrass Sundown, Simple Syrup, and Crème de Cocoa in a shaker over ice.
2. Shake until mixed.
3. Pour into chilled martini glass.
4. Over the back of a spoon, float a layer of Bailey's Irish Cream on top.

Two Bitch Spirits Ltd.

Eureka, Nevada

twobitchspirits.com
sip@twobitchspirits.com

Established
2016

Leadership
Joe & Lauren Luby, Owners
The Bitches: Miss Scarlett & Sage

Bourbon Berry Booya

This first batch of Two Bitch Spirits Bourbon has notes of anise which are enhanced by the blueberry anise simple syrup in the Two Bitch Bourbon Berry Booya. It's a cooling and refreshing way to enjoy bourbon during the dog days of summer!

Submitted by: Joe & Lauren Luby, Owners of Two Bitch Spirits Ltd.

Serve in a cocktail glass

Ingredients:
- 1 ounce blueberry anise infused simple syrup*
- 2 ounces Two Bitch Bourbon Whiskey
- 1 ounce freshly squeezed lemon juice
- Lemon zest
- Splash of soda water
- Ice

Preparation:
1. Add all ingredients to a shaker with ice.
2. Shake to frost.
3. Strain into cocktail glass. (Can also be served over ice.)
4. Garnish with lemon zest or wedge.

*Blueberry Anise Infused Syrup
Ingredients: 1 cup blueberries, 1 tablespoon Anise Seed and 1 cup of water -- **Instructions**: 1). Combine Anise, blueberries, sugar and water in a saucepan set over medium heat, bring to boil. 2). Reduce heat, simmer 15 minutes, stirring occasionally. 3). Let mixture cool then strain syrup through a fine mesh strainer into a mason jar or bottle. 4). Refrigerate. (Lasts up to one week.)

Bourbon Berry Booya

by Two Bitch Spirits

Venus Spirits

427 Swift Street, Suite A
Santa Cruz, California 95060
(831) 427-9673

venusspirits.com
info@venusspirits.com

Established
2013

Leadership
Sean Venus

Unusual Behavior

The unusual pairing of bourbon with tropical notes results in a perfectly balanced cocktail.

Submitted by: Sean Venus (creator of this cocktail)

Serve in a coupe

Ingredients:
- 1 ½ ounces Wayward Whiskey Bourbon
- 1 ounce lemon juice
- ¾ ounce pineapple juice
- ½ ounce vanilla spice syrup*
- ¼ ounce Orgeat
- 2 dashes Absinthe
- 2 dashes Peychaud's Bitters
- Pineapple wedge
- Luxardo cherry

Preparation:
1. Combine all ingredients in a cocktail shaker and fill with ice.
2. Shake until chilled and strain into a coupe.
3. Garnish with a pineapple wedge and Luxardo cherry on a bamboo pick.

*Vanilla Spice Syrup - 1 cup water, 1 cup sugar, ½ vanilla bean, ½ teaspoon nutmeg, ½ teaspoon cloves, ½ teaspoon allspice and zest from ½ an orange. Combine all ingredients in a saucepan and simmer for 10 minutes. Strain and cool.

Unusual Behavior

by Venus Spirits

Whiskey Acres Distillery Co.

11504 Keslinger Road
DeKalb, IL 60115
(844) 494-4753

whiskeyacres.com
info@whiskeyacres.com

Established
2013

Leadership
Jim Walter, Jamie Walter and Nick Nagele, Co-Founders

Whiskey Acres Bourbon Slush

Submitted by: Whiskey Acres Distilling Co.

Serve in a 12 ounce rocks glass

Ingredients:
- 9 cups water, divided
- 3 black tea bags
- 2 cups sugar
- 12 ounces of frozen lemonade concentrate
- 6 ounces of frozen orange juice concentrate
- 2 cups of Whiskey Acres Bourbon
- Ginger ale

Preparation:
1. In a small saucepan, bring 2 cups of water to boil.
2. Add tea bags and allow to seep for 10 minutes.
3. Discard teabags and stir in sugar until completely dissolved.
4. In large container, combine tea/sugar mixture, lemon and orange juice concentrates, water and bourbon.
5. Pour into a flat Tupperware (or similar) container and freeze for at least 4-6 hours (overnight if possible).
6. Serve using an ice cream scoop.
7. Top with a splash of ginger ale.

Whiskey Acres Bourbon Slush

by Whiskey Acres Distilling Co.

Wiggly Bridge Distillery

441 US Route 1
York, Maine 03909

wigglybridgedistillery.com

Established
2012

Leadership
Dave and David Woods

Fools Rush In

One of the unique parts of this recipe is the use of Maine Gold Bourbon Maple Syrup. Wiggly Bridge partnered with a maple syrup business in Maine. Used bourbon barrels were given to a local maple syrup company which made a bourbon barrel aged syrup. The barrels were then given back to Wiggly Bridge where they will be using them to create a uniquely maple infused product.

Submitted by: Wiggle Bridge Distillery

Serve in a rocks glass

Ingredients:
- 2 ounces Wiggly Bridge Bourbon
- ½ ounce Maine Gold Bourbon Maple Syrup
- 3 Drops (¼ teaspoon) vanilla extract
- Dash Angostura Bitters
- Orange zest
- Sprig of rosemary

Preparation:
1. Put all ingredients other than rosemary sprig in a cocktail shaker.
2. Shake.
3. Strain over ice.
4. Garnish with rosemary sprig and serve.

Fools Rush In

by Wiggly Bridge Distillery

Wilderness Trail Distillery

4095 Lebanon Road
Danville, Kentucky 40423
(859) 402-8707

wildernesstrailky.com
inquiries@wildernesstrailky.com

Established
2013

Leadership
Pat Heist and Shane Baker, Co-Owners

Summer Trail

The perfect blend of sweet and sour that tastes great year round.

Submitted by: Jerod Smith

Serve in a highball glass

Ingredients:
- 1 Part Wilderness Trail Kentucky Straight Bourbon
- 1 Part Frozen Lemonade Concentrate
- 1 Part Pulp Free Orange Juice
- 2 Parts Spring Water

Preparation:
1. Add frozen lemonade concentrate to pitcher.
2. Mix in 2 parts spring water and 1 part remaining ingredients using lemonade container as measuring cup.
3. Makes six 10 ounce servings.
4. For a refreshing frozen drink, substitute ice for spring water and mix in the blender.

Woodinville Whiskey Co.

14509 Woodinville Redmond Road NE
Woodinville, Washington 98072
(425) 486-1199

woodinvillewhiskeyco.com
info@woodinvillewhiskeyco.com

Established
2010

Leadership
Orlin Sorensen and Brett Carlile

WOODINVILLE
— • *handcrafted small-batch spirits* • —
WHISKEY CO.

La Abuela

Submitted by: Louis Morales/Taylor Shellfish for Woodinville Whiskey

Serve in a rocks glass

Ingredients:
- 2 ounces Woodinville Straight Bourbon Whiskey
- ½ ounce Licor 43
- 2 dashes of Angostura Bitters
- Orange zest
- Luxardo cherry

Preparation:
1. Combine ingredients in a rocks glass.
2. Stir.
3. Rub orange zest on the rim.
4. Add Luxardo cherry, skewered between a slice of orange rind.

La Abuela

by Woodinville Whiskey Co.

Wyoming Whiskey

100 South Nelson Street
Kirby, Wyoming 82430
(307) 864-2116 (ext. 1)

wyomingwhiskey.com

Established
2006

Leadership
Brad & Kate Mead and David DeFazio, Co-Founders

Brown & Gold Derby

Submitted by: Jesse Brown of the Cowfish "The Most Dangerous Bartender in Wyoming"

Serve in a rocks glass

Ingredients:
- 2 ounces Wyoming Whiskey
- 1 ounce fresh grapefruit juice
- ½ ounce fresh lime juice
- 1 ounce local Lander Honey Lemongrass Simple Syrup*
- 1 bruised sage leaf (place sage leaf in plastic bag and use muddler tool to bruise it by muddling it)

Preparation:
1. Add all ingredients into glass.
2. Stir.
3. Garnish with bruised sage leaf and serve.

*Lander Honey Lemongrass Simple Syrup Recipe
Bring one cup water, one cup honey and two stalks of lemongrass cut into ½ inch pieces to a boil for 15 minutes. Let cool and store in refrigerator.

Bonus Cocktail from Author Steve Akley

Steve Akley

steveakley.com
info@steveakley.com

Established
1968

Leadership
Steve Akley, Author, Podcast Host, Publisher of Bourbon Zeppelin

THE
BOURBON
SHOW
ABVNETWORK.COM

Bourbon Slush

This was a favorite at summer barbecues, parties and family gatherings when I was a kid. This is incredibly popular anytime I share it on Instagram.

Submitted by: Steve Akley (via his mother Sandy)

Serve in a highball glass

Ingredients:
- 1 can orange juice concentrate
- 1 can lemonade concentrate
- 3 cans* of water
- 1 more can* of water with 3 teaspoons unsweetened/powdered Lipton Ice Tea crystals in it
- 1 can* of bourbon
- Mix together and freeze overnight

Preparation:
1. Mix all ingredients together in a container (a one gallon plastic ice cream pail works great).
2. Freeze overnight (ingredients will freeze into a snow cone-like consistency).
3. Spoon into a highball glass and enjoy.

Can = Using one of the concentrate cans as a unit of measurement

Bourbon Slush

by Steve Akley

Resources

Websites of Featured Distilleries

I encourage you to learn more about these businesses and what makes them so special. To make your job a little easier, here's a recap of the websites for each:

2bar Spirits – *2barspirits.com*

Boone County Distilling Co. – *madebyghosts.com*

Bouck Brothers Distilling – *bouckbros.com*

Bourbon 30 Spirits Craft Distillery – *itsbourbon30.com*

Cockpit Craft Distillery – *cockpitdistillery.com*

Copper Fiddle Distillery – *copperfiddledistillery.com*

Cutwater Spirits – *cutwaterspirits.com*

Dark Corner Distillery – *darkcornerdistillery.com*

Detroit City Distillery – *detroitcitydistillery.com*

Distillery291 – *distillery291.com*

DogMaster Distillery – *dogmasterdistillery.com*

Dry Diggings Distillery – *drydiggingsdistillery.com*

FEW Spirits – *fewspirits.com*

Grand Traverse Distillery – *grandtraversedistillery.com*

Glacier Distilling – *glacierdistilling.com*

Honeoye Falls Distillery – *hfdistillery.com*

Hotel Tango Artisan Distillery – *hoteltangowhiskey.com*

Indian Creek Distillery – *staleymillfarmanddistillery.com*

Kings County Distillery – *kingscountydistillery.com*

Liberty Call Distilling – *libertycalldistilling.com*

Liberty Pole Spirits – *libertypolespirits.com*

Mad River Distillers – madriverdistillers.*com*

Motor City Gas Whiskey Distillery – *motorcitygas.com*

Myer Farm Distillers – *myerfarmdistillers.com*

OOLA Distillery – *ooladistillery.com*

Painted Stave Distilling – *paintedstave.com*

Rabbit Hole Distilling – *rabbitholedistilling.com*

Ranger Creek Brewing and Distilling – *drinkrangercreek.com*

Red Eagle Distillery – *redeaglespirits.com*

Reservoir Distillery – *reservoirdistillery.com*

St. Augustine Distillery – *staugustinedistillery.com*

San Diego Distillery – *sddistillery.com*

Silverback Distillery – *sbdistillery.com*

StiL 630 Distillery – *still630.com*

Striped Pig Distillery – *stripedpigdistillery.com*

Stumpy's Spirits Distillery – *stumpysspirits.com*

Sugar House Distillery – *sugarhousedistillery.net*

Syntax Spirits – *syntaxspirits.com*

Taconic Distillery – *taconicdistillery.com*

Timber Creek Distillery – *timbercreekdistillery.com*

Tom's Foolery Distillery – *tomsfoolery.com*

Town Branch Distillery – *townbranchbourbon.com*

Two Bitch Spirits – *twobitchspirits.com*

Venus Spirits – *venusspirits.com*

Wiggly Bridge Distillery – *wigglybridgedistillery.com*

Whiskey Acres Distilling Co. – *whiskeyacres.com*

Wilderness Trail Distillery – *wildernesstrailky.com*

Woodinville Whiskey Co. – *woodinvillewhiskeyco.com*

Wyoming Whiskey – *wyomingwhiskey.com*

Photo Credits

All photographs in the sections of each business featured have been utilized with permission from the respective companies with the following exceptions:

OOLA Distillery
OOLA Exterior and King Max Cocktail – Nicole Candi (Creative Brain/OOLA Distillery)

Striped Pig Distillery
Chucktown Sunrise Photo – Courtesy of Laurey W. Glenn / **Southern Living Magazine**

Stumpy's Spirits
Old Monroe Peach Lemonade Cocktail Photo – Keeven Photography

Sugar House Distillery
Mountain West Manhattan Photo – Darby Doyle (*abourbongal.com*)

Steve Akley's Bonus Recipe
Bourbon Slush – Renée Howe

About the Authors

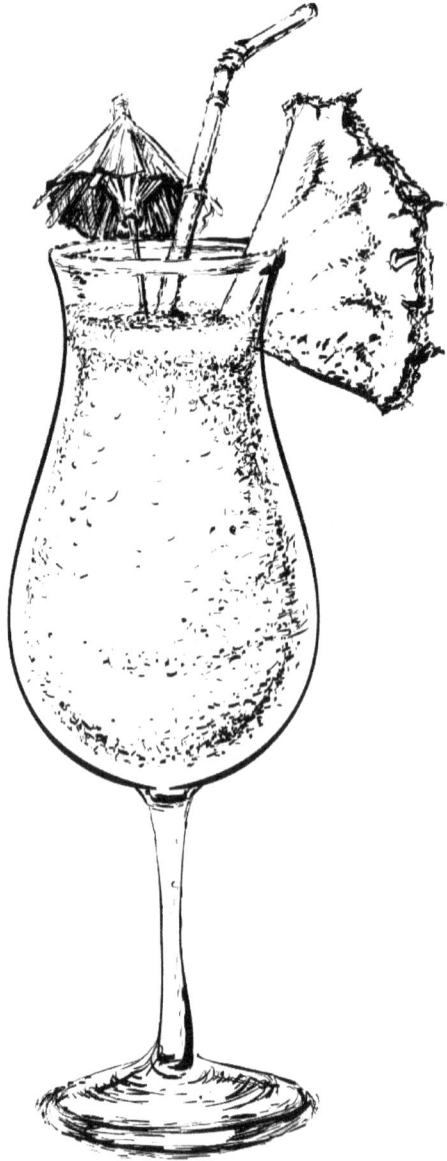

About the Authors

Steve Akley

Steve today and as a grade schooler meeting Andre the Giant

Steve Akley is a lifelong St. Louis resident. His approach to writing is very simple. He knows his passion comes from topics he enjoys so he sticks to what he knows best. In addition to books, he also publishes a monthly email magazine called Bourbon Zeppelin and is a cohost of two popular bourbon-themed podcasts, The Bourbon Show and The Bourbon Daily.

He maintains an author's page on Amazon.com. Just search his name on the site. He can be reached via email: info@steveakley.com.

Find Steve on Social Media

 & @steveakley & Steve Akley

About the Authors (continued)

Lee Ann Sciuto

Lee Ann, aka Punky the Intern, has known Steve since she was 9 years old. Besides helping Steve with the Bourbon Zeppelin, or a new book, she keeps busy trying to keep up with her daughter. She currently lives in St. Louis with her husband, daughter, and dog.

Steve's Other Works

Small Brand America
Special Bourbon Edition

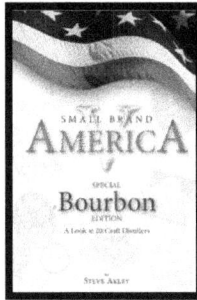

In ***Small Brand America V***, author Steve Akley explores small companies making a name for themselves with a truly American original: bourbon. Each has a little bit of a different take on making America's favorite distilled spirit. Inevitably, you will find yourself wanting to learn more about the companies and a desire to try their product(s).

Bourbon Mixology Series

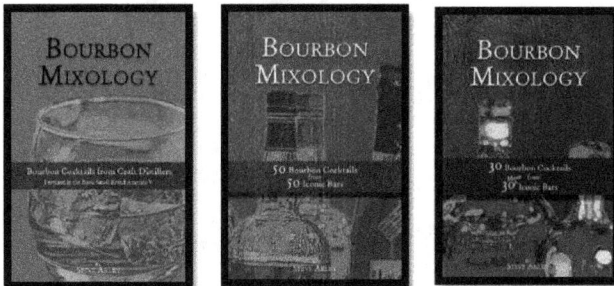

Be sure to check out the other offerings in Steve's **Bourbon Mixology** series!

Special Thanks

Much Appreciation for Those That Helped

To my wife Amy for her help in editing this book.

Thanks to our daughters Cat & Tessa for just being themselves.

Hats off to Mark Hansen (*mappersmark@gmail.com*) for the great cover design. He's the greatest graphic artist you will ever find!

Shout out to Steve's friend Renée Howe for modeling the Bourbon Slush.

The following individuals from the featured companies not only couldn't have been nicer, without their help this book would not have been possible:

Kent Rabish/Grand Traverse Distillery, Heather Bean/Syntax Spirits, Colin Spoelman/Kings County Distillery, Joe Fenten/Dark Corner Distillery, Nathan Kaiser/2bar Spirits, Pete Weiss/Town Branch Distillery, Calder Curtis/Cockpit Craft Distillery, Carol Ann Coughlin/Taconic Distillery, Maddie Rowley/Timber Creek Distillery, Ron Gomes/Painted Stave Distilling, Cole Levy/Detroit City Distillery, Jerod Smith/Wilderness Trail Distillery, Laura Stumpf/Stumpy's Spirits Distillery, Zachary Bouck/Bouck Brothers Distilling, Ashley Amato/Verde, Lauren Fallert/Verde, Lauren Riggleman/Silverback Distillery, Mark McDavid/Ranger Creek Brewing and Distilling, Seth Dettling/Big Escambia Spirits, Amanda Woods/Wiggly Bridge Distillery, Teal Schlegel/Honeoye Falls Distillery, Molly Thorvilson/Glacier Distiling, Lorilei Bailey/Tom's Foolery Distillery, Lissie Stagg/Reservoir Distillery, Veronica Stivers/Rabbit Hole Distiling, Kat Spellman/Woodinville Whiskey Co., Jim Hough/Liberty Pole Spirits, Mimi Buttenheim/Mad River Distillers, Nicole Ganz/Cutwater Spirits, Jason Horn/FEW Spirits, Joe and Lauren Luby/Two Bitch Spirits, Chris Stellar/Aurum Sierra, Joe Myer/Myer Farm Distillers, Katie

Breden/Hotel Tango Artisan Distillery, Trent Tilton/San Diego Distillery, Sara Barnes/Boone County Distilling Company, Lauren Long/Venus Spirits, The DogMaster Distillery team, The Striped Pig Distillery team, Rich Lockwood/Motor City Gas Whiskey Distillery, Nick Nagele/Whiskey Acres Distilling Co., David Weglarz/StilL 630, Kristen Olson/Distillery 291, Philip McDaniel/St. Augustine Distillery, Scott Pugh/Bourbon 30 Spirits Craft Distillery, Eddy Eckart/Red Eagle Distillery, Sailor Retro/Indian Creek Distillery, James Fowler/Sugar House Distillery, Bill Rogers/Liberty Call Distilling, Nancy Hernandez/Copper Fiddle Distillery, Laurie Wilhoit/Copper Fiddle Distillery and Kirby Kallas-Lewis/OOLA Distillery

Lastly, lots of love for Steve's father, Larry Akley. He's always with us in spirit.

THE END

www.ingramcontent.com/pod-product-compliance
Lightning Source LLC
Chambersburg PA
CBHW072012290326
41934CB00007BA/1057